NORA ROBERTS LAND
Selected as one of the Best Books of 2013 alongside Nora Roberts' *DARK WITCH* and Julia Quinn's *SUM OF ALL KISSES*.
--*USA Today Contributor, Becky Lower, Happily Ever After*

"It {NORA ROBERTS LAND} captures the best of what I love in a Nora Roberts novel..."
--*BlogCritics*

"...finding love like in the pages of a Nora Roberts story."
--*Publisher's Weekly WW Ladies Book Club*

FRENCH ROAST
"An entertaining ride...{and) a full-bodied romance."
--*Readers' Favorite*

"Her engaging story and characters kept me turning the pages."
--*Bookfan*

THE GRAND OPENING
"Ava Miles' Dare Valley world is a wonderful place to visit..."
--*Tome Tender*

"The latest book in the Dare Valley series is a continuation of love, family, and romance."
--*Mary J. Gramlich*

THE HOLIDAY SERENADE
"This story is all romance, steam, and humor with a touch of the holiday spirit..."
--*The Book Nympho*

THE TOWN SQUARE
"Ms. Miles' words melted into each page until the world receded around me..."
--*Tome Tender*

COUNTRY
Heaven
COOKBOOK

AVA MILES

www.avamiles.com
Ava Miles

ISBN-13:9781499246773

To my grandma, Lanone, for teaching me how to cook, for showing me how to infuse love and joy into food, and giving me this piece of her now that she's passed on. I know if there's a kitchen in heaven, you're there making pies, cinnamon rolls, and peanut brittle for everyone, waiting for me.

Dear Readers and Foodies Alike!

This cookbook is a special companion to the single title novel, COUNTRY HEAVEN, the first in my Dare River series. Readers have enjoyed the scrumptious recipes I wrote for the book so much that I wanted to share them all together with some **extra family recipes NOT included in the book.** Who wants to page through their book or scroll through their e-reader to find a recipe anyway? Not me. As you may already know, I spent some time working as a chef, so I just love to weave food into my novels. Included here are recipes for my famous spongy cornbread (I have the secret!), gingerbread waffles (oh my heavens), and our chocolate chip pie (yes, you read that right).

The cookbook entries describe my heroine's reflections about her grandmother, who taught her to cook. I can relate. My grandma taught me to cook too. See, real life is like fiction! If you haven't read the book yet, this is a great chance to see how beautifully food is woven into the story between my sassy heroine, Tory Simmons, and my steamy country singer, Rye Crenshaw. I've also included **an extended excerpt** of COUNTRY HEAVEN at the end for your enjoyment.

Reviewers and readers have been going crazy over COUNTRY HEAVEN, which delights my heart. Here's just one review to give you an idea. "If ever there was a contemporary romance that rated a 10 on a scale of 1 to 5 for me, this one is it!" The Romance Reviews

And if you don't know what the story is about, well, here's your bird's-eye view:

When famous—and infamous—country singer Rye Crenshaw saunters into the diner where she cooks, Tory Simmons is certain she's got him pegged. He's a bad boy who indulges himself in all things, women included. But while she couldn't care less about country music or arrogant men, Rye makes her an offer she can't refuse when he asks her to be his private chef on his multi-city concert tour. The job is the answer to all her prayers: it will clear out her debt and finance the fresh start she desperately needs.

Rye is certain his sassy new cook is the last woman who'd ever tempt him, but spending time with the wholesome girl next door will do wonders for his damaged public image, whether she likes

being forced into the spotlight or not. Her food also happens to be the best he's ever eaten, both comforting and seductive. But spending time with Tory on the road shows him a new side to her—one that's as impossible to resist as her food. And when an emergency in his family whisks him home, he does the one thing he's never risked: he lets a woman into his heart...

Soon the emotions Rye faked for the tabloids become all too real, but will the country heaven he's found in Tory's arms survive in the real world?

I hope you enjoy the cookbook and the extended excerpt! I have THE COUNTRY HEAVEN SONGBOOK available as well since the book features Rye's songs (lyrics only mind you; I'm not Carrie Underwood yet). His music is pure poetry and is designed to inspire. I hope these recipes inspire you as well and that you are able to share them with your family and friends. Thanks so much for picking up this cookbook!

Lots of light,

Ava

PS If you like to have fun, enter contests to receive free books, and win gift cards, come connect with me through my newsletter and on Facebook and Twitter. Feel free to post any pictures of you making these recipes on my Facebook wall. My readers love to share recipes and pictures of food like I do. I'm also on Goodreads and love to share giveaways there too, so I hope you friend me to kick off the party.

RECIPES FROM COUNTRY HEAVEN

TABLE OF CONTENTS

Recipes from COUNTRY HEAVEN 11

Basic Cornbread Recipe 11

Truck Driver Pancakes 12

Lemon Meringue Pie 13

Tory's Creamy Vegetable Sauce 15

Sugar Cookies...16

Tory's Chocolate Chip Pie 17

Cream Puffs (or French Eclairs a la Tory) 18

Chinese Pot Roast 19

Gingerbread Waffles 20

Lady Baltimore Cake 21

Fan-tabulous French Toast... 22

Tory's Mouthwatering Lasagna.. 23

Ava's Family Recipes.. 24

The Miles Chocolate Sheet Cake 25

Ava's Easy Stuffed Apple Crepe 27

Decadent Chocolate Pudding.. 28

Candied Nuts... 29

Buttermilk Biscuits 30

Ava's Bourbon Sweet Mashed Potatoes 31

Ava's Dry Rub for Mouthwatering BBQ.................................... 33

Ava's Easy Peasy Garlic Bread 35

Ava's Fried Chicken a la Grandma... 37

Ava's Rosemary lemonade 40

RECIPES FROM COUNTRY HEAVEN

BASIC CORNBREAD RECIPE

Grandma Simmons had one traditional cornbread recipe she would make either sweet or savory, depending on Grandpa's mood. When he had a bad day, she'd make maple cornbread to sweeten his disposition. When he was feisty—or she wanted him to be—she'd make Mexican, adding grated cheddar cheese and jalapeños from our garden. The secret is the buttermilk, the frothy elixir that makes it super moist and rise like crazy. You can make more variations than maple or Mexican cornbread. Be bold. Experiment. Find out what makes your man sweeter or spicier. Believe me, deep down, you know.

1 cup cornmeal
½ tsp. salt
½ tsp. baking soda
2 tsp. baking powder
1/3 cup flour
2 tbsp. melted butter
2 eggs
1 cup buttermilk (fresh or from powder)

Combine the dry ingredients. Add the butter, beaten eggs, and buttermilk. {For maple: add 1/3 cup maple syrup. For spicy: add 2 Tbs. chopped jalapeños and 1 cup cheddar cheese.} Stir. Pour into a greased pan and bake for 20 minutes at 450 degrees. A cast iron skillet works best.

Tory Simmons' Simmering Family Cookbook

TRUCK DRIVER PANCAKES

Being the cook at Diner Heaven for nearly thirty years, my Grandma Simmons dealt with some pretty mean truck drivers. They'd come in off the highway with bloodshot eyes and bark at the waitresses. One particular man was so mean, she fixed him a special stack of pancakes, certain they'd improve his disposition. Grandma believed the way to a man's heart was through his stomach, but she didn't think food's power stopped there. She talked about the emotional reactions all people had to food. The mean truck driver wasn't growling anymore after eating her special pancakes, so she added them to the menu with great success.

1½ cups flour
1 tsp. baking soda
¼ cup sugar
½ tsp. salt
¼ cup cocoa
2 eggs, beaten
1 cup milk
½ cup butter, melted and cooled
½ cup chocolate chips

Combine the dry ingredients. Add the eggs, milk, and butter. Stir. Add the chocolate chips. Shape into pancakes on the griddle and cook. Serve with maple syrup or bittersweet chocolate ganache.
Tory Simmons' Simmering Family Cookbook

LEMON MERINGUE PIE

My Grandma Simmons made incredible pies. There are two mediums you have to master to do the same. A flaky crust is essential. Here's a tip if you're making it from scratch: use Butter Crisco™. It really does make an incomparably flaky, golden crust. But you can't stop there. You have to make a filling that doesn't crack or weep. Lemon meringue is my favorite of all the pies she used to make. The secret to her meringue was the extra egg whites she used to create those four inches of magic that swirled on top as puffy as clouds. Add fresh lemon zest, and you have a real winner—a comforting yet tangy treat for a hot, humid day. I've never met a person whose mood didn't improve after having a slice of this pie. Its magic is potent.

Pie Crust

1 crust for the bottom (you can buy a prepared crust or make one from scratch). Here's our family recipe.

1 c. flour
½ tsp. salt
1/3 c. regular or Butter Crisco™
¼ c. cold ice water (we put ¼ in a 1 c. measuring cup and add ice to it)

Mix until incorporated (not too much, but just until it comes together). Then roll the dough into a circle on a floured surface. Lay into the pie plate and flute the edges by pinching the dough on the top and sides between your two index fingers.

Lemon filling:

1½ cup sugar
3 Tbs. cornstarch
3 Tbs. flour
Dash of salt
1½ cup boiling water
3 egg yolks beaten

2 Tbs. butter
½ tsp. grated lemon peel (fresh is best)
1/3 cup lemon juice
1 tbsp. lime juice

Mix sugar, cornstarch, flour, and salt. Add boiling water. Cook over stove until the mixture boils and thickens, about 2 minutes. Temper the egg yolks with the hot mixture and add to the saucepan. Cook for 2 additional minutes and remove from the stove. Add butter, lemon peel, and lemon juice. Pour into crust.

Meringue

5 egg whites
½ tsp. vanilla
¼ tsp. cream of tartar
½ cup sugar

Beat egg whites with an automatic beater until they form peaks. Slowly add sugar until dissolved.

Add meringue to the pie and seal it to the corners. Cook at 350 degrees for 12-15 minutes until meringue is lightly brown.

Tory Simmons' Simmering Family Cookbook

TORY'S CREAMY VEGETABLE SAUCE

I've never cared for vegetables. I suppose I should say plain vegetables. Whoever said they were good for you really ruined my life. There's a whole host of other foods I'd rather be eating. Being from the Midwest, we didn't do much to our veggies. So I decided to try something new one day. One of my favorite veggies is asparagus. Alone, I'm not sure I'd care for it, but I've learned one of life's essential truths—heavy whipping cream makes everything better. If calories bother you, stop reading now. But if you're like me and willing to indulge every once in a while, give this a try. You'll never look at asparagus again in the same way. Oh, and here's a helpful hint: the sauce also works wonders on green beans.

1 tsp. olive oil
2 cloves garlic, mashed
1 cup heavy whipping cream
½ tsp. fresh ground pepper
¼ cup feta cheese
¼ tsp. Greek seasoning
2 tbsp. Brandy
1 tsp. lemon juice (fresh)

Heat the olive oil and sauté the garlic until brown. Add the next four ingredients until the cream bubbles around the sauce pan and reduces. Add the brandy, and if you're lucky enough to have a gas stove, dip it toward the flame. The mixture should ignite and further reduce the cream. Add the lemon juice. Cook 1 more minute. Remove and serve over your vegetable of choice.

Tory Simmons' Simmering Family Cookbook

SUGAR COOKIES

When my parents died, I was only twelve, and my grandma must have wondered what to do with me. When I came to live with them, they hadn't had children in the house for decades, but I never felt like I didn't belong. Grandma brought me into her magical world of cooking, which helped heal my grief. One of the first recipes she introduced me to was sugar cookies. Now most people make these at Christmas, but Grandma, well, she believed you could make them any time of year. So, we'd make the dough, and then pick from the cookie cutters she'd been collecting for years. If we didn't have the shape we wanted, we'd improvise and make our own, using frosting to decorate instead of colored sugar. For me, it was better than cutting out paper dolls on a rainy day.

1 cup butter
1 cup sugar
3 eggs
3½ cup flour
1 tsp. soda
2 tsp. cream of tartar
1 tsp. vanilla

Cream the butter and sugar. Add the eggs. When the mixture is fluffy, add the remaining ingredients. Blend well. Refrigerate until the mixture is cold and hard. Roll out into the desired thickness. Cut into shapes. Bake 375 degrees for 10-12 minutes. Decorate.

Tory Simmons' Simmering Family Cookbook

TORY'S CHOCOLATE CHIP PIE

When it comes to comfort food on the sweet side, there's nothing better than combining a chocolate chip cookie flavor in a flaky pie crust. I like to add a little cocoa for extra bite. This sucker is pure decadence and perfect for Sunday dessert with fresh whipped cream or heated to warm on a school night. You can barely keep your eyes open after the first bite, least of all form a complete sentence. It makes even the most sensible senseless. My friend served it when her difficult mother-in-law came for a weekend visit. She gave her guest a piece every day she was there and said it was the only time the woman didn't find something to complain about. So, if you're in need of comfort food, chocolate with your pie, or you want to shut someone up—this pie is for you.

3/4 cup butter
1/2 cup sugar
1/2 cup brown sugar
3 eggs
1/2 cup flour
2 tbsp. cocoa
1 cup chocolate chips
1 cup pecans

Cream the butter and sugar. Add the eggs. Mix. Add the flour and cocoa. Stir until combined. Add the chocolate chips. Pour into an already baked pie crust. Cook at 325 degrees for 50 minutes.
Tory Simmons' Simmering Family Cookbook

CREAM PUFFS (OR FRENCH ÉCLAIRS A LA TORY)

When I was little, I watched Gone with the Wind *with my grandma. The movie captured my imagination. The women seemed so elegant in their hoop skirts, dancing the Virginia Reel with men sporting wickedly handsome slim mustaches. Houses like Twelve Oaks with their curved staircases seemed a dream. Being an only child, I frequently imagined friends like Scarlett or Melanie for my tea parties. Using my grandma's lace-edged napkins, I'd serve what we termed French éclairs. They were actually cream puffs, but again, we used our imagination. Scarlett wouldn't eat cream puffs. Depending on how much time my grandma had, sometimes we'd serve the éclairs with vanilla pudding, which we called French custard. Other times, I simply settled for French Chantilly cream. Back then, I used Cool Whip with a dash of ginger. Now, I can make all these things from scratch. But as a child, those cream puffs were magical. And my imaginary friends in their fine gowns were always pleased.*

1 cup water
1 stick of butter
1 cup flour
4 eggs

Boil the water and butter until the latter melts. Add the flour and mix, forming a yellow paste. With a wooden spoon, add 4 eggs, one at a time, and beat well. Drop with a tablespoon onto a greased cookie sheet. Bake at 400 degrees for 30 minutes. Slit the cream puffs and fill with custard or cream, depending on your preference. Or fill with something else that sounds good to you. These airy, golden brown pastries work well with many fillings.

Tory Simmons' Simmering Family Cookbook

CHINESE POT ROAST

Being from the Midwest, my family cooked a lot of roasts for dinner. Obviously, the same old, same old, gets old. So, we'd make a Chinese pot roast every now and again. I'm not sure what made it Chinese. Perhaps the ginger and soy sauce. Heaven knows, we added potatoes to the mix, not rice. But it was always a winner. The meat's flavor simply explodes in your mouth, and the broth makes the best juice for the potatoes. It's a simple dish to make with some lead-time—one of those all-in meals that's perfect for families or days when you're on the run. My grandma was fond of fixing this before we'd go to church. We'd return to a splendid smelling house, set the table, and feast.

1 chuck roast, about 4 lb.
2 garlic cloves, minced
A dash of nutmeg and cinnamon
2 tbsp. brown sugar
1 tbsp. sherry or red wine
¼ cup soy sauce
1¼ cup water
3 peeled and sliced carrots
3 potatoes, peeled and cubed
1 celery stalk, sliced
2 tbsp. cornstarch

Marinate the meat in the next six ingredients for at least 3 hours. Place the meat in a roasting pan at 325 degrees for 2 hours. Add the vegetables 45 minutes before cooking time ends. Voila!
Tory Simmons' Simmering Family Cookbook

GINGERBREAD WAFFLES

I don't know what it is about breakfast, but starting off the day right with a good one gives me a better attitude. Granted, my grandma raised me to never leave the house without breakfast. Eggs, pancakes, and waffles were routinely on the table when I came downstairs before leaving for school. I once commented that I wished we could have gingerbread more often one Christmas since I loved my grandma's Gingerbread men, so she found this recipe. These waffles always make me happy. They're a special treat—like unwrapping presents on Christmas morning.

½ cup molasses
6 tbsp. oil
1 cup milk
2 beaten eggs

Mix together and add the following dry ingredients together in a separate bowl and then add to the liquid ingredients:

2 tsp. baking powder
½ tsp. baking soda
1 tsp. ginger (fresh is best)
½ tsp. cinnamon
4 tbsp. sugar
2 cups flour

Cook in a waffle iron for 4-6 minutes until golden brown. Serve with a lemon sauce or maple syrup.

Tory Simmons' Simmering Family Cookbook

LADY BALTIMORE CAKE

My Grandma made a lot of cakes, but my favorite was her Lady Baltimore—an old school, spongy white cake that you don't see too much anymore. Maybe it was the name, which reminded me I was special, but I always chose it for my birthday. She'd frost it with a mouth-watering buttercream frosting in the colors I liked best, adding cabbage roses in the corners. Other times, I'd select a "shape" cake, like an elephant or a horse, and she'd cut the cake into pieces and reassemble it, transforming a normal cake into a magical creation. By the time the cake was punctured with candles, it was a work of art. And while you were sad to see the magical cake disappear, you never thought twice about eating it. With one bite, it hooked you.

¾ cup butter
2 cups sugar
3 cups sifted cake flour
3 tsp. baking powder
½ tsp. salt
½ cup milk
½ cup water
1 tsp. vanilla
6 egg whites

Sift the cake flour with the salt and baking powder. Cream the butter and sugar. Whip the egg whites to stiff. Combine milk and water with vanilla. Mix half the flour mixture and milk/water mixture into the creamed butter and sugar. Stir. Repeat the process. When blended, gently add the egg whites in batches until thoroughly mixed. Pour into a buttered and floured pan. Bake 25 minutes at 350 degrees.

Tory Simmons' Simmering Family Cookbook

FAN-TABULOUS FRENCH TOAST

Everyone has something they crave when they're sad or away from home. Being halfway around the world in rural Africa, I realize mine is French toast. Its power to lighten your spirit, soothe your worries, and make you feel closer to home is magical. My Grandma started the tradition by bringing day-old French bread home from the diner where she worked. We were always looking for ways to use it. This recipe worked like a charm—and we never tired of it. Dress it up with a good cup of coffee or mimosa and enjoy its scrumptiousness.

1 loaf of French bread
¼ cup butter
2 eggs
1 2/3 cups milk
Pinch of salt
3 tbsp. sugar
1 tsp. nutmeg

Slice the loaf into pieces and butter both sides. Line a buttered pan with the bread slices. Beat the eggs. Add the milk and pinch of salt. Stir. Pour over bread and sprinkle with nutmeg. Chill for at least 1 hour (overnight is best). Bake at 425 degrees for 20-25 minutes until golden brown. Serve with warm maple syrup and a side of fruit. Strawberries are especially lovely.

Tory Simmons' Simmering Family Cookbook

TORY'S MOUTHWATERING LASAGNA

Every good cook has a signature dish. Even though I'm not of Italian heritage, one of my signature dishes is lasagna. The wonderful thing about cooking is that you can go anywhere in the world simply by cooking in your own kitchen. Since we didn't have any money to travel to mysterious places when I was a kid, I started cooking recipes from countries I wanted to visit. When I was first introduced to Italian cuisine, I felt that I'd found my second home. Their approach to food—simple, family style with fresh local ingredients—seemed to blend with my own vision of what makes a good meal. Serve it to your family with a good red wine. Light some candles. And celebrate togetherness.

2 packages sausage
1 lb. hamburger
6 cloves garlic
2 tbsp. Italian seasoning
1 can tomato paste
1 small can crushed tomatoes
1 carton of cottage cheese or ricotta
2 beaten eggs
1 tbsp. Parsley
¾ cup Parmesan cheese
Mozzarella cheese

Fry the meat and when cooked, add the garlic and Italian seasoning. Then add the tomato paste and crushed tomatoes. In another bowl, mix the eggs, ricotta, parsley, and Parmesan cheese. Boil the lasagna noodles in salt water until *al dente*. In an oil-coated pan, layer in two stages: noodles, meat mixture, creamy mixture, and then top with mozzarella. Bake at 375 degrees for 50 minutes until golden brown.

Tory Simmons' Simmering Family Cookbook

Ava's Family Recipes

Now on to the recipes NOT included in COUNTRY HEAVEN. These are from my family or my own personal ones. I hope you enjoy my reflections on them as well. Food is life to me, and I am so grateful to have learned to cook from my grandmother. She's passed on, but I know if there's a kitchen in heaven, she's there making pies and cinnamon rolls for everyone, waiting for me. Of course, my mom is an incredible cook too, but she had six kids so didn't have much time to teach me. But boy did I enjoy her food growing up. Now, I'm the one the family asks to frequently cook at our fun family reunions. Everyone has a favorite dish of mine, and I am happy to share all of these recipes here with you. May your table always be blessed and your life filled with flavor.

THE MILES CHOCOLATE SHEET CAKE

Let's start with dessert since my grandma wasn't a stickler for us having a sweet before dinner. On her last birthday, she had two pieces of cake—one for lunch and one for dinner—because she wanted to make she enjoyed as much of that cake as she could, knowing her health was failing. I remember my grandma making this recipe a lot when I grew up.

Now, every time I make this family recipe, people grab my sleeve and say, "This is the best chocolate cake I've ever had." I have to admit that I agree, and it proves one item I have learned about recipes. Only the really great recipes stand the test of time, and this old farm recipe from my family goes back likely a hundred years. It's perfect for a party, a picnic, or a church social. And get ready to hand out the recipe because people will ask.

1 c. water
4 tbsp. cocoa
2 sticks of butter

Bring these ingredients to a boil.

2 cups flour
2 cups sugar
1 tsp. soda
½ c. buttermilk
2 eggs
1 tsp. vanilla

Add the boiled chocolate concoction to the flour, sugar, and soda. Then add the remaining ingredients and mix with a blender. The mixture will bubble, but don't worry. It's supposed to. Pour into a greased and floured lipped cookie sheet and bake at 350 degrees for 15 minutes. Check with a toothpick. Remove the cake when the toothpick comes away clean.

Frosting

3 tbsp. milk
4 tbsp. cocoa
1 stick of butter
1 tsp. vanilla
4 cups powdered sugar

Save the saucepan you used for the boiled mixture (who doesn't like one less pan to wash?) and melt the cocoa and butter. Pour it over the powdered sugar, milk, and vanilla and beat. Pour the frosting over the cake when it's slightly warm from the oven. This makes it easier to spread. Then sit back, grab a fork, and dig in. Prepare to have your eyes flutter shut.

AVA'S EASY STUFFED APPLE CREPE

During the winter, I always seem to want something sweet and warm. One day I realized I wanted something meatier than a crepe, which I adore, and filled with apples. For some reason, I love cooked apples in the wintertime. So, I came up with this recipe. Now I make it just at the house or for guests. It's easy, fast, and flavorful. I hope you'll give it a shot to warm your tummies on a cold night.

2 eggs
1 cup flour
1 cup milk
¼ cup butter
2-3 apples sliced
1/3 cup sugar
2 tsp. cinnamon

Beat the eggs and then add the flour and the milk. This will appear like a thick crepe batter. Set aside. Heat the oven to 425 degrees since you're about ready to use it. Slice the apples as evenly as possible (a feat I had to master in our head chef's kitchen, but now I slack off). Melt the butter in a cast iron pan if you have it and add the apples, sugar, and cinnamon, stirring a couple of times to mix the ingredients. Cook until translucent and then add to the oven and cook there another 3-5 minutes. Remove the apples from the oven and pour the crepe batter on top. Cook for another 15-20 minutes until the crepe rises and turns a toasty brown. Then serve warm by itself or add some ice cream or whipped cream. It's also a great breakfast or brunch treat fyi, so experiment when you want to serve it. Whatever the time, people love it.

DECADENT CHOCOLATE PUDDING

This recipe is another winter favorite, but it's really incredible anytime. My mom made this a lot for us growing up, so it's a big comfort food at home now. My siblings even get a little homesick when I tell them I made it. ☺ It's also super versatile. I can turn this base recipe into anything I want. I can add raspberry essence to the top, making people groan, add hazelnut extract, inciting awe, or even cinnamon, creating surprise. Be daring!

2 cups milk/soy milk
1/3 cup cocoa
1/3 cup flour
¾ cup sugar or honey
2 egg yolks
2 tbsp. butter
1 tsp. vanilla

I am always experimenting with using more natural products, and yes, you can successfully use honey if you'd like. So here's the trick with chocolate pudding. Combine the flour and cocoa in the saucepan and add a little of the milk. Whisk. You want to make a paste. Why? No lumps. Aha! That's a little trick I've learned over the years. Then pour in the rest of the milk and stir until incorporated. Cook at medium heat until the pudding is thickening. Be mindful about the temperature because the milk can scald. When thick, temper the egg yolk and chocolate pudding and mix into the saucepan. Then add the butter and vanilla (and anything else your heart cries out for). Cook a couple minutes more. Pour into bowls or ramekins or anything else fun and have at it. Use whipped cream, dot with fresh raspberries, or even some candied nuts (recipe forthcoming). You won't regret it. Oh, and here's a secret. You can pour this into a cooked pie crust for an incredible effect as well. Nothing better than Chocolate Pudding Pie. Doesn't that sound just decadent?

CANDIED NUTS

As I continue to eat healthier, I adore cooking with nuts (sorry for those of you who are allergic). After experimenting with natural sugars, I also have found a way to have my sweet fix without using regular sugar. This recipe is so simple and tasty that you won't believe it. The maple syrup caramelizes on the nuts and makes them taste like caramel corn. Oh my! You can eat this alone or add them as toppings as I have mentioned before (like bourbon sweet mashed potatoes). Prepare to have people begging you for this recipe.

2 cups nuts (your choice)
2 tbsp. butter
½ cup maple syrup
1 tsp. vanilla
¼ tsp. of sea salt

Melt the butter in a saucepan and add the maple syrup and vanilla. Cook until it simmers (about 2-3 minutes) and then add the nuts, cooking another 2-3 minutes. Be careful not to burn this mixture. Pour out onto a lipped cookie sheet either lined with parchment paper or aluminum foil (cooking tip: less clean up, trust me). Then spread out the nuts until they are even on the cookie sheet and sprinkle the salt on top (this creates an incredible flavor). Bake in a 375 degree oven for 6-8 minutes. You do not want to burn the nuts, and it's easy to do (I might have done it once when I got busy with something else). When they come out of the oven, allow the nuts to cool. You will have to break them apart like hard candy in some places, but that's part of its charm (assuming your family doesn't gobble it off the cookie sheet like mine did). The nuts will not be hard until they cool fyi in case you want to sneak a taste, so don't worry. Then scoop up a handful or serve in a special bowl for guests. These babies go fast!

BUTTERMILK BISCUITS

Growing up in a small town in a family of six kids, my mom made buttermilk biscuits frequently. I can still see the old frosted 1970s glass she used to cut the biscuits into circles. Of course, we would all beg for some dough (I think it's one of my favorite raw doughs out there). Now, I make these when I am hankering for a home-cooked meal or simply want to have a biscuit with some special jam. These biscuits are special treats, and while they are simple, they make people smile.

2 cups flour
2 cups sugar
1 tbsp. sugar
¼ tsp. soda
2 ½ tsp. baking powder
1/2 tsp. salt
1/3 cup butter
3/4 c. buttermilk

Cut the butter into the dry ingredients until the mixture is crumbly. Then add the buttermilk and stir. Do not over mix. On a floured surface, roll out to ½ inch thick and then cut into circles with a glass (flour the rim). Place on a greased cookie sheet and bake at 450 degrees for 12-15 minutes. Serve warm if possible and enjoy!

AVA'S BOURBON SWEET MASHED POTATOES

I unabashedly love mashed potatoes. Growing up in the Midwest, we probably had them twice a week. There is nothing better than that creamy, buttery treat swimming in homemade gravy (the women in my family know how to make gravy, let me tell you, and I share our milk gravy for fried chicken so keep reading).

But I adore sweet potatoes too, but the only time we ever had them growing up was on Thanksgiving, and they were so candied, the caramel sauce stuck to your teeth (divine though). When I moved to the South, I kept being introduced to sweet potato casseroles. They were swimming in marshmallows and sometimes pecans, and while I loved them, one night as I was making dinner, I decided to try something simpler and faster. What about sweet "mashed" potatoes? And I had to kick it up, as my grandmother used to say, by adding a splash of bourbon. When I first tried them, I about swooned. Since then, I make them all the time. Some guests have come close to swooning as well, so let me tell you, if you are looking for a simple treat, give this recipe a try and prepare to have your taste buds knocked out of the park. Oh, and these are dairy-free, so if you're lactose intolerant or watching your dairy intake, these are for you!

sweet potatoes, peeled and quartered
honey to taste
1/2 tsp. salt
1/3 cup butter
1 tsp. cinnamon
1 tbsp. Bourbon

Every family is a different size, and so is every potato, which is why I am not going to give hard and fast measurements here! For you beginner cooks, you cannot mess these up, trust me. Peel and quarter the potatoes. Why quarter? Let me clue you in on a secret. It took me until I was an adult to realize they cook faster this way. It was a *duh* moment. Growing up, I was taught to cut them in half. Quartering cuts the boiling time down significantly. Place them in a pan and fill with water. Set it on the stove and boil. You will need to keep the lid on until the pot boils, and then vent after or they will overflow on the stove. Sad face here, but I have done it many times. Less clean up when you're prepared for it. When you can put a fork in the potatoes, they are done. Pour off the water. I use the lid to do this; some people use a colander. Use whatever works for you.

Then mix them with a beater until they are thoroughly mashed (if you like them lumpy, go for it). From there, add the butter and let melt. Mix more. Then add the salt and cinnamon. Mix. Now the honey. Do this in stages, tasting the mixture until it's to your liking. Everyone has a different sweet ratio. Once these are blended, add the splash of bourbon and serve hot. Trust me, you don't need anything to go on these babies. They are perfect as they are. Sometimes, I just eat a bowl of these for dessert with some candied nuts I whip up (yes I whip up candied nuts; my friends love me for it, and I'm sharing the recipe with you: keep reading). Voila! You have a simple masterpiece that is as flavorful as it is unusual.

AVA'S DRY RUB FOR MOUTHWATERING BBQ

BBQ has become one of my favorite niches. Growing up, we didn't really have it, but when I moved to the South, we came across it all the time, thank the Lord. Now seriously, there are intense debates about the best BBQ out there. I can only share that I am all about the dry rub and a good smoke. Yes, I have my own smoke box. I even bring back special woodchips from a place near my parents' house, now that they live down South. Men love me for that. They're like, "a BBQ chick?" Yes, that's me.

So, here's my signature dry rub recipe. I make it in double and triple batches and store it in either an airtight container or the freezer—wherever there is more room. I won't go into smoking your ribs since that's a whole different discussion, but I will tell you a secret. You don't need a smoke box. You can use tin foil. If you're interested, there's plenty of information on the Internet about how to do that. Most people don't have the time or inclination to smoke their own meat, and that's cool. This BBQ rub is so awesome that you won't feel like you're missing the smoke (of course it's better with the smoke, but anyone would guess that). Try this out and see what you think. It's one of my favorite recipes when I am having guests over during the summer. I often use baby back ribs with this rub, but see what meat tempts you.

2 tbsp. salt
2 tbsp. sugar
2 tbsp. brown sugar
2 tbsp. ground cumin
2 tbsp. chili powder
2 tbsp. pepper
1 tbsp. cayenne pepper

This recipe rocks because it's mostly a 2 tbsp. recipe, so it makes it easy to measure and dump (less cooking tools and clean up; yes, I use the same tablespoon over and over again). Some of the other rub recipes call for so many little baby measurements, you want to pull your hair out. Can you tell I like efficiency sometimes? Combine all of the ingredients and mix well. Rub onto the meat of your choice. I like to rub a meat at least the day before, if not two (beef and pork only; chicken and fish need less time). I do this on a large cookie sheet, lipped if possible. That way it's less messy. Then cook your meat up like you would usually and get ready to have that smoky sweetness knock your socks off!

AVA'S EASY PEASY GARLIC BREAD

I don't have a lot of rules, especially when it comes to cooking. So it will not surprise you that I don't believe garlic bread is only served with Italian food. Who made that rule? I make this recipe all the time when I want something special and easy. Garlic bread easy, you say? No way. Right, you were taught like I was growing up. You have to cut each slice vertically, which is like thirty freaking slices, and then butter each side until your fingers want to fall off. We always made garlic bread to go with the lasagna we serve for Christmas Eve. Remember Tory's lasagna recipe earlier in the cookbook? Yeah that's our family one. Shh...Well, I hated to make garlic bread after all that work. Then I ran across a guy who blew me away with his sheer efficiency. He cut the French loaf horizontally and spread his garlic butter in one fell swoop. Duh. Seeing that changed my life. Cook this recipe on the grill—the other thing he taught me—and you'll never go back to the old way.

Whole bulb of garlic

1 cup butter

Salt to taste

Real garlic you say? Yes! Do it. It's so easy and makes life more beautiful. But first, set out your butter so it can soften. Now, cut the top of the bulb off, set in a over-safe baking dish, and sprinkle olive oil on top. Bake in a 325 degree oven for about 45 minutes. You house is going to smell amazing, so enjoy. Then when it's done, squeeze the garlic from each clove into the bowl of softened butter. This is the messy part. No getting around it, but it's worth it. Now mix until it's integrated, being sure to crush the roasted garlic as well as you can. Add a little salt to taste. Then spread onto the French bread in one pass! By the way, Rhett Butler Blaylock, one of the characters in THE GRAND OPENING, actually cut the bread horizontally too (of course the heroine thought he'd done it wrong, but I knew better). Butter both sides. Yes, you can. Grill on medium heat for about 3-4 minutes a side. Your grill will fire as some of the butter melts on the coals, but it's unavoidable. I cry when a piece of garlic falls through the cracks, but I always hope The Grill Fairies eat it. Then cut the bread into squares and serve immediately. Your life will never be the same!

AVA'S FRIED CHICKEN A LA GRANDMA

One of my sisters suggested I share this next recipe. I taught her how to make fried chicken when she was visiting one time—the way our grandma taught me. Our grandma made the best fried chicken, and it didn't hurt that she always had fresh chickens from either her farm or someone else's in their small Midwest town. I tried to make fried chicken when I moved out on my own. The first try was miserable. I couldn't "get it right." Have you ever had that happen? So the next time I came to grandma's house I asked her to make it so I could watch her. The ingredients for fried chicken are easy, so what I'm sharing is how I have mastered making it like our grandma. My best friend from Memphis says it's the best fried chicken he's ever had, which from a town with food like Memphis, that's an incredible compliment. Fried chicken is what I call my "last meal" if I had a choice about it. For me, it's pure comfort, simple, heartfelt, and packed with pure flavor. We make mashed potatoes to accompany it, and something not a lot of people make anymore: milk gravy. I'm sharing that recipe too below in case you want to try it. I hope you practice this recipe because I had to, but once you master it, you will be the talk of the town.

Fried Chicken
chicken pieces
vegetable shortening
flour
pepper
salt

Melt the shortening in frying pan (not one of those no-stick kinds; they don't work for fried chicken). You're going to want to melt enough to have about one quarter inch in the pan. You're going to want the pan to be on medium high heat, but not smoking. Chicken sears best with heat to start. Now, on a plate, sprinkle some flour. The amount depends on the amount of chicken you have. Could be

½ cup to start. You may need more. I sometimes have to add more. No worries. And if you have leftover flour, you can just toss it in the garbage. It's just flour. Add salt and pepper to taste. Yes, use your finger. ☺ Then coat both pieces of chicken in the flour mixture and place in the heated frying pan. Then leave it to sear. The biggest lesson I learned from our head chef was "don't play with your meat." This is gospel, let me tell you, and is true for all kinds of meat.

Check the chicken and once it has a good sear, turn over. Check your grease level; you may need to add more vegetable shortening. When you've turned the pieces over (turning in the order you arranged them in the pan usually), put a lid on it, but vent it (no lid? Use a cookie sheet.). You want there to be some air, but you also want to cook the inside of the chicken. You should see a golden crispy sear forming. That's what you're looking for. After the chicken has turned translucent, uncover, and keep cooking. The crispy outside softens a bit while covered, but the open air brings it back. When the chicken is done, put it on a plate and place it in a warm oven while you make the gravy. Don't clean your frying pan. That's the pan you're going to use to make milk gravy with.

Marvelous Milk Gravy
Milk
Flour
The frying pan with crunchies and oil

That's it, you ask? Just milk and flour? Yes. Gravy is an art form. If you have a significant amount of grease in the pan, use a paper towel and blot it until you have about 1 tbsp. or so remaining in the pan. Add a tbsp. of flour to start and then scrape the pan. That's right. Scrape it. You want the crunchies and the flour to blend into a messy roué. Then you're going to want to add some milk in a slow stream until it starts to thicken. Then let it simmer. The good news about a roué is that you can always add more milk if it's too thick. Just be mindful of not adding *too much milk* because you cannot just throw flour in there and not get lumps. If it is too runny, you'll need to make a flour/water paste and add that to the mixture and hope for the best. ☺ I've had to do it, but it's never ideal. I can say that my family never cared if a few lumps came through.

My sister and I even loved the lumpy gravy so much one time that we spread it on French bread. It is ridiculous! Again, there's always a place to experiment. Once you have the gravy done, pour into a gravy boat if you have one and serve the chicken, mashed potatoes, and whatever else you made. Then sit back and eat as your heart expands. This meal is about love, comfort, and finding the flavor in life.

AVA'S ROSEMARY LEMONADE

(or The Hollins Family Lemonade from COUNTRY HEAVEN)

Especially during the summer, I sometimes get a craving for lemonade. That tart, crisp taste hits the spot, especially when I am gardening. Well, I have been making my own lemonade since I had my own place (and the real kind this time, not the powder version like we had growing up). But I was in the garden one day, and well, inspiration always strikes out of nowhere when it comes to cooking and...drinking (did I mention I'm a mixologist too?). My enormous rosemary bush seemed to speak to me then, and I listened. Yes, I hear plants. Call 911. Seriously, I thought, what would rosemary taste like in lemonade? I cut off a nice sprig, went inside, and added it to the water and sugar concoction I use to make simple syrup. And do you know what? It more than hit the spot. It knocked it out of the ballpark. I have since served this lemonade at afternoon lunches or teas at my house or with people I know who don't drink alcohol for brunch. It has become a signature of mine, and I hope you try it out. Of course, I mentioned this lemonade in COUNTRY HEAVEN and that it was a family recipe of Rye's family. But it was really mine. I didn't think to add the recipe in the book, but here it is.

1 cup lemon juice

Rosemary-Infused Simple Syrup
2 cups water
honey
large rosemary sprig

Let's start with the lemon juice. Fresh is best. Shocker, I know, but you can use a high quality frozen lemon juice if you're in a hurry. I won't tell. I have. Add the lemon juice to your pitcher. Now, onto the simple syrup. Take out a saucepan and add the ingredients(except for the lemon juice, remember?). Set to boil, watching carefully. If you didn't know it, honey raises the boiling temperature. When the mixture boils, the honey will create some foam. Don't worry about that. Once it boils, turn down to a simmer and cook the mixture for about 15 minutes. This ensures that rosemary flavor is infused. When finished, remove the rosemary. Add ice to the pan to cool it down (you're going to add it to water anyway, so why not cut down on the cooking time this way?). Fill your pitcher with ice (lemon juice should already be there). Then pour the simple syrup in. If it's still warm, the ice will melt it (thus ensuring you won't crack your pitcher).

This recipe makes 2 quarts, so if you need to add more water to reach that mark, go ahead. (And here's a tip: taste it before you serve since all lemons are different in tanginess). You can garnish the glass with a sprig of rosemary. Trust me, you are going to enjoy this drink. Oh, and if you're a gardener like me, try adding other herbs. Basil rosemary is delicious, and you can use the same recipe. Experiment. Innovate. That's what I love about cooking. It is never the same.

Well, that's it for the recipes! I hope you enjoy many happy meals with them at your table. May they warm your heart as well as your belly.

And if you enjoyed these cookbook entries, please take a peek at this extended excerpt of COUNTRY HEAVEN...

ℙROLOGUE

Nashville's Disadvantaged Children's Association's Annual May Day Charity event at one of the city's finest country clubs didn't have a whiff of disadvantage, in Rye Crenshaw's opinion.

Ice sculptures of unicorns and cherub-faced children were dripping in the hot sun on the plush buffet table. The silver flatware fairly blinded him, and the plates gleamed so brightly they looked like they'd been shined with furniture polish. At least the food appealed to him, the succulent beef tenderloin and slow-roasted pork being sliced delicately by black-tie waiters while others carried around silver trays with champagne, mint juleps—this was Nashville, after all—and delicate canapés of crab and caviar. An assortment of European cheeses from bleu to goat caught his eye, and his stomach grumbled. Food was one of Rye's greatest pleasures in life, and he loved indulging in it.

Thank God the only thing the chairperson of the DCA wanted from him today was his presence, his pocket book, and for him to take some pictures with the disadvantaged kids they'd brought to the event. No live performance singing songs from his new album, *Cracks in the Glass House*, which continued to rise to the top of the charts.

His had been a wild ride to stardom after a childhood spent without any autonomy. Now, he did exactly what he wanted, went where he wanted.

Except on days like today, when his manager, Georgia Chandler, arranged for him to attend a hobnob charity event. He liked giving back to the community and hated seeing kids treated poorly, but he didn't like being put on display like some zoo animal.

And he downright hated hoity toity events like these, having had his fill of them growing up in blue-blood Meade, Mississippi, before breaking the family tradition of being a lawyer in the family practice to pursue country music.

Of course, his family hadn't liked that one bit. And events like these made him think about them...and how they'd disowned him when he stepped out of line.

Georgia made her way toward him, wearing a leopard-print

mini skirt, a black blouse, a black cowboy hat, and five-inch black cowboy boots that left punctures resembling bullet holes in the finely manicured lawn as she meandered through the crowd.

"Are you ready to work your magic?" she asked when she reached him.

"Yes," he said, and joined her to stroll through the crowd of Nashville's finest, being stopped for an occasional autograph or a more personal proposition from some of the elegant ladies in attendance.

He had just finished shaking hands with the mayor when his cell phone vibrated in his jeans, and since Georgia was busy chatting with the politicos, he stepped away. He dug his smart phone out of his pocket, and his heart just about stopped...

It was the number from his family's house, which he hadn't stepped foot in for five years.

A spear of fear drove straight into his heart.

"Hello?" he said, hurrying away from the crowd, the sun beating down on his black cowboy hat.

"Rye, I hope this is a convenient time to call," she said.

Mama? The reason she was calling must be dire. She must have gotten his number from his sister, the only person in his family with whom he still communicated. And just as he remembered, Mama's tone was so cold it could have kept the ice sculptures from melting.

"Of course," he woodenly replied. Manners must always be observed.

"Good. Well, then. I've learned that you plan to attend Amelia Ann's graduation from Ole Miss, and I'm calling to tell you not to come."

Anger sparked inside him, hot and fierce. "She's my baby sister, Mama, and I'll come see her graduate if I want." It wasn't like he'd planned on sitting with them anyway.

A brittle laugh echoed on the line. "I thought you might say that. Rye, when you left this family and turned your back on everything we stood for, your Daddy and I made it crystal clear you were to have no contact with any of us again. And wasn't it a surprise to hear that you've been secretly in contact with Amelia Ann for some years now. Well, I forbid it."

One of his songs suddenly erupted from the speakers, and he had to put his finger in his ear to hear her. "Too bad. She's an adult now, and I'll see her if I want."

Amelia Ann had reached out to him five years ago when he'd been disowned, sending him an email, and they'd kept up a secret correspondence ever since. When she started at Ole Miss, they began talking on the phone now and again, and Rye had even visited her periodically. But they'd been careful, both of them well aware that Mama wouldn't approve.

"Rye, I won't have my baby sullied by your lifestyle or your unconventional belief system. Amelia Ann will take her rightful place back home in Meade after graduating, and she'll marry a fine Southern gentleman and have babies, just like Tammy has done."

Yeah, his older sister, Tammy, had toed the line. She was so much like Mama they might as well be twins.

"Mama, I'm going to that graduation," he said, an edge in his voice.

"If you do, Rye, or if you have any more contact with her at all, I will disown her too."

The punch of that threat rolled across his solar plexus.

"I won't tolerate another rotten apple in my barrel."

"You wouldn't," he said, even though he knew she would. Mama was the kind who would eat her own young at any provocation.

"Try me, Rye. You didn't use to underestimate me."

No, he hadn't. Her weapons were sharp and unforgiving. And he had the scars to prove it. "Fine," he said. "I won't go to her graduation." It cost him to consent, but he couldn't bear to see Amelia Ann hurt. She had a gentle, loving heart, which is why she loved her black sheep brother against the family's wishes. They would find a way to be in touch.

"And no more phone calls," Mama added, as if reading his mind. "I'll be monitoring her phone bill in the future."

Christ.

"Don't mess with me on this, Rye. I've spoken to Amelia Ann, and she has accepted my dictate. You'd best do the same."

His sister had caved? The hurt of never again seeing her bright smile or hearing her laugh on the phone almost brought him to his knees. "You're a goddamn mean-spirited bitch," he spat.

"I love you too, son. Bye now."

The phone went dead, and he fought the urge to hurl it across the yard. Goddammit! He punched the air instead, wanting to strike out at something, anything.

He didn't often feel helpless in his life anymore, but he did now. And it was pure hemlock, hearing the utter hatred in Mama's voice again, like he was a whelp she'd brought into the world and hoped would simply disappear from existence.

Getting out of this charity event was the first order of

business. He didn't care if it was early. Georgia could write them a fat check to smooth over any complaints.

He texted her to say he was leaving and that he'd explain later. As he reached the side entrance to the country club's lobby, a heavily built man grabbed his arm.

"Leaving so soon?" the man drawled, his mouth an ugly sneer. "A hot shot like you can't even stay to help disadvantaged kids?"

Since he'd been harassed by strangers before, he knew better than to reply. He tried to step around the guy without comment, but the man was bold and blocked him. Rye could guess at the reason for that boldness when the stench of alcohol wafted over him.

"Best get out of my face today, boy. I'm not feeling too nice today."

"You're just some country whelp." Little did this man know how thick the blue blood ran in Rye's veins, even if he went out of his way to conceal that fact. "You don't belong among good family folk," he continued.

"Your opinion."

The man only scratched his fat belly with his other hand. "You're a good-for-nothing son of a bitch, and you don't deserve to be here."

The words echoed in Rye's head, but this time it was his mama's voice he heard. The towering inferno of rage erupted inside him, spewing like a dormant volcano that had just come awake after sleeping for years. He shoved the man out of his way, and the man fell to the side and started howling.

Rye immediately reached to help him up, but the guy jerked away and yelled, "He hit me! Rye Crenshaw hit me."

Of course, a crowd gathered at the noise, the man yelling about how violent Rye had been. How he wasn't fit to be around children. And wouldn't you know it, a few of the disadvantaged children the association had brought for the event teared up and cried like in some frickin' Dickens novel.

Camera phones flashed everywhere.

He was screwed.

Striding out of the country club, hounded by the man's shouts, he waited for his truck to come around to the valet stand and called his lawyer on the way home to tell him what had happened so he could call the police and give Rye's account. He'd bet the farm the man was going to press charges. Good God, the whole rigmarole made his head swim.

By the time he made it home to Dare River, Twitter had

exploded with pictures of the fat man writhing on the floor, Rye standing over him looking dark and foreboding. And then there were the accusations.

Rye Crenshaw Punches Innocent Man at a Charity Event
Rye Crenshaw Mean to Children.
Rye Crenshaw Violent Around Kids.

He threw his phone against the wall of the den, the crack of it breaking doing nothing to comfort him. Georgia would be wild to talk to him, as would the rest of his staff, but he couldn't handle that now. Grabbing a bottle of Wild Turkey, he headed out to the river and stood by the bank. But the usual delight he took at seeing the water turn to diamonds in the light was gone.

His reputation had just taken a devastating blow. He might cultivate a bad-boy image, but what was being said in the media would shock his fans. And it wouldn't matter if the police didn't press charges. Like the old phrase went: a picture is worth a thousand words.

Even he knew that.

And just as he was starting his tour at the end of the month.

His career could be in trouble, but all he could think about was that his baby sister, his precious heart, was lost to him.

He hung his head and sank to his knees by the river.

Chapter 1

Over a month later...

The run-down appearance of Diner Heaven just outside Lawrence, Kansas, didn't concern Rye. Everyone knew diners were hidden food gems.

Through a grime-encrusted window, he could see a lone redheaded waitress bustling around under harsh fluorescent lights, wiping down white countertops. That the diner looked to be empty was a bonus. He wouldn't have to contend with any of his country music fans and their worried glances, pinched mouths, or flat-out nosy questions about whether he'd *plumb lost his mind* at the charity event on May Day. The man whom Rye had shoved, a wealthy businessman, had pressed charges for assault and blabbed to anyone who would listen about how Rye didn't have family values and was too wild to be around "decent people."

He'd had to go to the downtown police precinct for questioning, and there were pictures all over the media of him alongside the men in blue. Few cared that the police hadn't charged him, finding little evidence and observing the man had been drunk.

Tonight, he'd fled the stage after his concert and was immediately attacked by a rabid female fan and swarmed by journalists with cameras who asked him rude questions while shoving cameras in his face. Over a month after *The Incident*, they were still asking him if he had anger management issues, if he needed counseling, and whether he hated kids and families.

So here he was, craving a little comfort food and peace since he'd recently fired his tour cook—another disaster he didn't want to think about. And he was crammed into a beat-up muscle car, two decades old if it was a day, that he'd borrowed from a member of their local crew, wearing a ball cap instead of his black Stetson. Trying to be all *incognito-like*.

No one ever saw him without his cowboy hat, so he should be able to fly beneath the radar. Plus he met the restaurant's high standards. He had on shoes *and* a shirt. Bully for him.

The sooner he got inside, the sooner he could get back to the tour bus and start the drive to the next concert stop. He slammed the car door, rubbing the bite mark on his neck from the overzealous fan. Darn kids read too many vampire books these days. A cat the color of his beloved Oreo cookies shot past him.

And then he saw the striped tail.

He lunged for the car, but it was too late. A menacing hiss punctuated the silent parking lot, and a filmy spray misted his clothes. He gagged at the rotten smell and pinched his nose.

Rye knew Kansas had a reputation for being rural, but seriously. His stomach growled. God, he was rank, but he was *starving*! Grateful the wind wasn't behind him, he prayed the waitress would have seasonal allergies and a plugged nose.

He pulled the cap lower, hoping he could pass for an innocent college student with his jeans and black T-shirt. He snorted. Innocent he wasn't.

The door chimed when he eased it open, and he nudged the doorstop down with his foot. Maybe fresh air would help. The air conditioner blasted more of a tepid tropical breeze than a meat-locker chill anyway. He sighed, even over *eau de skunk*, he could pick up the heavenly odors of garlic, onions, and grilled meat.

The middle-aged waitress gave him a once-over like a bad private investigator keeping tabs on her target. She was wearing a gold uniform with a monogram of clouds and a halo under her name tag. Myra. He nodded a greeting and shuffled forward. "I'm just gonna head to the men's room to see if I can wash off this skunk's stink. It got me in the parking lot."

Her nose twitched, and then her face scrunched up. "Oh, good heavens!" She bustled over, pressing a white lace handkerchief to her tired face like he had cholera or something. "That darn thing. We've had two customers sprayed this week. Bill can't catch it, and I hate to see it shot. I watched Pepé Le Pew growing up."

A cartoon was stopping her from getting rid of it? Well, didn't that beat all?

"Don't bother to try washing it off. It won't help," she said.

"I'm sorry," he said. God, he must be the unluckiest son of a bitch on the planet.

"It *sure* is rank." She shifted on her feet, the handkerchief morphing like a sock puppet as she breathed through it. "Umm... We were about ready to close. Our cook's cleaning the grill." Her eyes darted to the kitchen.

Her voice had the flat, articulate cadence of a TV anchorperson. People in the Midwest teased him about his slow drawl, but he was simply too lazy to finish pronouncing the end of most words. He hoped he could tone down the Southern in his voice tonight, though. The last thing he needed was for this situation to end up in the tabloids.

"I'm sorry to put you out, but I wouldn't ask if I wasn't starving. I couldn't get here any earlier." He kept his head down, looking at her white shoes. Her right shoelace was untied.

"All right, but only because our skunk got you."

Whew. "Wonderful. What do you recommend, Myra?" Rye eased into a cracked fake red leather booth.

"Why don't I see what our cook can whip up for you? Tory's awfully inventive." She bit her lip as her nose wrinkled. "She'd be more inclined if you smelled better. We used Febreze on the last person. It works as good as tomato juice and isn't as messy. Do you mind?"

Might as well give it a try. "Sure. Go ahead."

She disappeared around the counter, and then popped back up with a blue bottle. He'd been sprayed with a few things in his life, but this was new. The things a guy did for a good meal. He stood up and forced a smile as she edged toward him slowly, like the smell might be contagious. She pinched her nose and went to work, the handle cranking. Mist filled the air, making him cough. She was thorough, he'd give her that. Now Rye was covered in Febreze *and* skunk. Things couldn't be peachier. He'd have to burn the clothes.

Myra's eyes were watering, so at least he wasn't the only one suffering. Setting the bottle down, she flexed her hand. "That's better. Amazing what this stuff can do. I keep it around the house. Wait, I got some on your face." She took her handkerchief and wiped his cheek like he was a kid. He jerked his head back, his eyes meeting hers for the first time.

Her own narrowed and then popped open as wide as the silver dollars his granddaddy used to give him for Christmas. "My God! I'd know those long-lashed eyes anywhere." Her pale, heart-shaped face transformed. "You're Rye Crenshaw! You had a concert tonight. I wanted to go, but I couldn't find anyone to cover my shift. There were some tickets available last minute because of what happened last month." She pressed her hand to her mouth. "Oh, I'm so sorry. I shouldn't have said that."

Rye fought back a growl. Like he didn't know some of his more conservative fans thought he'd crossed the line and were dumping their tickets.

"I'm sorry. I know I screwed up," he muttered.

Hadn't he practiced saying the words every morning since *The Incident*? Georgia, his manager, had written them in bold red letters on yellow legal paper and taped it to his bathroom mirror in the tour bus. They'd made an official announcement about the drunken man harassing him, but the media kept running those pictures of the disadvantaged kids crying over and over again. So, he kept apologizing—even though it burned his ass each and every time.

Myra lifted the blue bottle in her hand. "This would...ah, make a funny commercial. Maybe you could become a Febreze spokesperson." She shrugged. "It would be a family item. Might help restore your reputation."

Like hell. He and Georgia hadn't figured out how to turn the tide of negative press, but he doubted an air freshener endorsement would do it. If Corona, a brand that suited his bad boy image to a T, had decided he was too much of a liability, why would some hygiene-concerned wife and mother buy this Febreze stuff because of him?

"I'll mention it to my manager." He lied to be polite.

His stomach gave a hungry gurgle.

She looked at his belly like there was a monster about ready to break out. "I'll get Tory." She scurried off toward the swinging kitchen door, her sensible shoes squeaking with each step.

He took a seat again.

A woman with jet black hair peered through the glass hole in the door just before Myra sailed into the kitchen. He caught whispers of heated conversation and then the door slammed open, smacking the wall, and a petite woman charged toward him with a hand towel over her nose. She had on faded jeans with a hole in the knee and a smudged white apron over a red T-shirt. Her big eyes peeked out at him from under a messy pageboy haircut.

"We close at midnight, and it's..." She lifted her wrist to look at her watch. "Exactly seven minutes to—not enough time to make you something. I don't care if you're that infamous singer everyone's talking about or what. I don't even listen to country." She studied him for a moment. "You don't look anything like your picture."

Rye's mouth lifted at the corners. "That was the idea. Look, I'm sorry you're about ready to close. Tonight hasn't been a party for me either." He lifted the damp, Febrezed T-shirt clinging to his chest, hating the flowery, skunky smell of it. "I didn't do anything to your skunk." He dug out his wallet and thumbed through it. "I'll pay you five hundred dollars to stay open and feed me."

Her eyes narrowed a fraction, and she put her hands on her slim hips. "You think throwing your money around here will get you a meal?" Her gaze zeroed in on the red mark on his neck.

He didn't cover it with his palm like some embarrassed teenager, but defending himself seemed a good idea. "Some fan decided to make a spontaneous audition for Bram Stoker's *Dracula* after tonight's concert. Sunk her teeth into my neck before I knew what hit me."

Stories made people comfortable, so he pretended he was giving an interview. He'd charm the pants off Barbara Walters to get a meal tonight.

"Security went crazy, dragging the woman away kicking and screaming. Luckily she didn't break the skin, or I'd have to worry about rabies and communicable diseases. Can you imagine? After that, I burned rubber and came here. According to Yelp, you're the best diner in town. Over a hundred reviews with a 4.5 rating. Impressive."

She didn't look amused—or like she believed him for a second. He did have a reputation with the ladies, after all.

"Nevertheless, it's late, and I'm tired. I'll need more

incentive than that."

Myra, who had trailed out after the spunky chef, gasped. "Tory! What has gotten into you?"

He couldn't contain the grin. He wasn't often treated poorly by people—present scandal aside—so she was a welcome change. Fame had a way of making people kiss his ass faster than he could say dandy. He settled back into the booth, which was about as uncomfortable as stadium bleachers.

"I like your spunk, and the reviews on Yelp did say a meal here is worth every penny. What would you say to a thousand?"

Her eyes fluttered before narrowing again. They were as green as his favorite beer bottle and almond-shaped. So, she hadn't thought he'd agree to up the ante. Wasn't that interesting?

"That works," she replied.

The amount was over-the-top, but it would be good PR. Stories like this tended to get out. His people could spin it into something good. He was helping out some ladies who'd served him a great meal.

Myra clutched her hands, muttering something he couldn't make out.

Rye counted out ten crisp one-hundred dollar bills. "So, what can you make me?" He caught the shake in Tory's fingers before she shoved the money into her pocket.

She crossed her arms in a cocky stance. "What do you like?"

Oh, did he have some inventive responses to that one. "I'm a meat and potatoes kind of guy, but after Myra's praise for your intuitiveness, I'll take whatever you want to make me."

She started tapping her tennis shoe on the linoleum. "You like chicken fried steak?"

He gave her a smile. "Yes, Tory, I do. Thanks." How had his life gotten to the point where he was casually spending a grand on a meal at a greasy spoon?

She turned and walked past Myra, who was shaking her head like a disapproving schoolmarm. "Not a word," the pixie said.

Still muttering to herself, Myra poured him a glass of tea, which he immediately sweetened. Then she picked up her dishrag and started scrubbing the stainless steel counters by the cash register, keeping at it until Rye could see her reflection in them. As he waited for his food, he flapped his damp shirt against his chest, hoping it would air dry. The stickiness against his skin was cold and uncomfortable.

Fifteen minutes later, he heard a shout from the kitchen. Myra raced back and came through the doors moments later with a heaping plate. She smiled when she set it in front of him.

"I hope you like it."

The chicken was fried to perfection, all golden and crisp. Rye closed his eyes as the smell and steam wafted up to him, taking a moment to be grateful. Food always pleased him, and tonight he needed the comfort of it more than usual. He cut into the chicken fried steak, eyeing the buttery mashed potatoes and creamed beans. The first bite was just as advertised. Heaven. He fought the urge to gobble the whole plate up like a hog. Some things were worth savoring. The food was incredible, but then again, he'd always thought diner food had something on those snooty five-star restaurants where his mama used to drag them.

He ate slowly as his belly warmed and filled. The noise in his head—like New York City at rush hour—faded away. If he didn't know better, he'd say there was something special in this food. He hadn't been this calm and focused since *The Incident*.

Myra hurried over with a pitcher of tea and refilled his glass. He dumped in half a cup of sugar and stirred.

"Someone's got a sweet tooth." She grabbed his empty plate. "Do you want lemon meringue pie or carrot cake for dessert?"

Rye leaned back against the booth, sated. "If it's as good as the meal, how about a slice of both? I nearly licked my plate."

"Sure thing. Tory might be sassy, but she's a damn good cook. She's just more stressed than usual. Her grandfather died four months ago, and she's trying to make things work with the hospital bills, mortgage, and school. That's why she pushed you for more money for the meal, I think." She grimaced. "I wanted to tell you as a way of apology. She's a good girl."

"It's no problem."

Myra slid his newest CD out of her apron and shyly extended it toward him with a pen. "I was listening to your music earlier tonight since I didn't get to go to your concert. Would you autograph it for me?"

He studied the cover. *Cracks in the Glass House* showed him swinging his guitar like a nine iron at a glass house covered in spider fractures. They'd taken a hundred pictures of him before declaring they had the winner. Personally, he couldn't tell why this one was any better than the ninety-nine others.

"I'd be happy to. What would you like me to write?"

"For continued courage."

He tapped the ballpoint on the table. "You having a tough time too, Myra?"

Her face turned red. "I have two kids in college and another graduating next year. Always seems to be another bill in the mail. That's why I understand Tory. She's a survivor. Sometimes I wish I had her courage."

"I'll bet you have more courage than you think," he said as he signed the CD.

Myra touched the case reverently after Rye pushed it toward her. "About what happened in Nashville..." she whispered. "Those of us who love your music know the media is blowing this whole thing out of proportion. I hope you find a way to deal with the bad press. Your music inspires us." Her face beamed like soft lamplight. "I'll get your dessert now."

He watched her go, his fingers gripping the table. How could he undo that moment of idiotic recklessness? If he hadn't pushed the man aside, the guy would never have fallen. Yes, there had been reason enough for his moodiness, but it wasn't any of *People* magazine's business. He never talked about where he was from and his life before country music, and it was that life that had risen up to kick him in the nuts once again. And break his heart. Oh, Amelia Ann.

His career was all he had left, and right now he needed some positive publicity, and he needed it pronto.

Strategies rolled around in his mind as Myra brought him dessert. The lemon meringue had to be about four inches tall. This meringue melted like cotton candy in his mouth, and the tangy lemon filling made him think *za za zing*, lifting his spirits again. Then came the carrot cake. The cream cheese frosting coated his tongue, and the cake—loaded with raisins, shredded carrots, and nuts—hit his taste buds like a flavor bomb. His eyes fluttered shut, and he groaned, chewing slowly. God, sometimes food was as great as sex.

The cake crumbs called to him, and he swiped them up with the last trail of frosting before pushing his plate away. He couldn't remember eating anything that good since he'd been at his Granny Crenshaw's house.

And all from the hands of a cranky, down-on-her luck cook.

"Down-on-her luck," he muttered.

An idea started to piece itself together like the first verse of a song. Why leave everything to Georgia or fate? He could kill two birds with one stone. Eat well *and* improve his image.

"Myra, could you have Tory come on out?"

"Sure, Mr. Crenshaw. I'll be right back."

She left before he could tell her to call him Rye. Or how he planned to thank Tory for the incredible meal, which was worth every penny of the thousand dollars she'd negotiated, just like Yelp had said.

***

Tory scrubbed the grill in furious strokes, ignoring her aching muscles. God, she hated cleaning it, and twice in one night royally sucked.

And all for that stinking redneck—literally. She didn't care what Myra said. Febreze might be magical stuff, but it did *not* completely obliterate skunk smell.

The grayish dishwater coated her hands and soap and grease bubbles danced and popped across her skin. She closed her eyes, hoping to relax. Her head was too full, her thoughts like a sprinter racing relays from one mark to the next.

She couldn't ignore the facts anymore. She was on a one-way path to bankruptcy. The thousand dollars would help, but she'd give Myra half. Her family was having troubles too.

What was happening to her? Part of her couldn't believe she'd hit the guy up for more money, but seeing him throwing the bills around like they were Monopoly money had set her teeth on edge. Why were the most undeserving the most successful? Seriously, every major media outlet had covered Rye Crenshaw's attack on that man, at an event for children, no less. Myra swore up and down the man had been inebriated, just like Rye had said in his official statement. Like she knew.

Deep down, Tory knew it wasn't just Rye's presence that had set her off. Another hospital bill had arrived in the mail yesterday, and the tight-knotted terror of that number at the bottom of the page had overwhelmed her. Her grandpa hadn't had supplemental insurance, so Medicare hadn't covered everything.

Scrubbing faster, she told herself she'd get through. Maybe she could pick up a second job. She curled over the sink, making her lower back twinge. When? Now that the semester had ended, her time at the diner began at breakfast and, after a short break in the afternoon, she was back until midnight. With her student loans and the mortgage to the family house she couldn't sell, the bank wasn't about to give her any more money. She'd have to take out another credit card, and pray she could handle the payments and horrible interest rates.

"Tory?" Myra called when she came through the door. "Mr. Crenshaw wants to see you."

"Isn't he finished yet? I'm beat."

"I know, dear. I need to get home too. He's just had his

54

dessert. I think he just wants to pay his compliments."

She was gone before Tory could reply. Finishing off the grill, she wiped her hands on a faded blue dish towel. There were new black streaks across her apron, but what did she care?

Her knees hurt like she had a sprain when she trudged out of the kitchen. Even though he sure seemed to like food, he was fit, built. Broad shoulders. Firm chest. The ball cap looked strange on him after the pictures she'd seen of him in a cowboy hat, but she liked it. Without the cowboy getup, he was attractive—someone she would have looked at twice in a bar. His ash blond goatee framed some seriously chiseled lips. God she must be exhausted to be thinking like this. He was the last person she'd ever go for... And Lord wasn't it funny that she'd even think of that—it was hardly like he'd go for her either.

"You liked the meal?" she said when she reached his booth.

His mouth kicked up. "More than any I've had in a long time. I wanted to thank you."

Maybe it was because she'd spent the break in her shift packing up her grandpa's liquor cabinet, but Rye Crenshaw's voice made her think of the small batch bourbon her Grandpa drank before he got sick. All dark and smoky and...

What was it about good looking men and deep, throaty voices?

Okay, now she really needed to get to bed.

"If my granny were here, she'd ask you for the secret to your carrot cake," he said.

A man who punched people at charity events was asking her about secret ingredients? Wasn't that a first? "I usually peel the carrots, but I can't remember if I did today. Maybe it added texture." Yes, she'd been that tired.

"Oh..."

He blinked rapidly, making her notice his heavily lashed eyes. To say they were hazel wasn't enough. The browns, golds, and greens reminded her of a forest at dusk.

"Myra said you wanted something," she said.

"Like I said, the meal was incredible. Best I've had in some time. Thank you."

Well, she could be civil too, when the situation called for it. "You're welcome."

"She tells me you've had some tough times recently. You're in school?"

Tory turned her head to glare at Myra, who ducked into the kitchen. The diner was quiet save for the whooshing of the swinging door and the hum of the fluorescent lights.

"She shouldn't have said anything."

"She was trying to explain your..."

"Bitchiness?" she supplied, a bit of laughter creeping into her voice.

Rye cleared his throat and broke eye contact for a moment. "I'd never use that word to describe a lady."

Wasn't he full of it? "Right."

"What I wanted to say is that I'm sorry for keeping you open. You have to go to school tomorrow?"

She shifted her feet to ease her back ache. "No, I'm off for the summer. I work here full-time now."

"You're at the University of Kansas, right?"

"Yep."

Rye reached for his dessert fork and tapped it on the table. "When does school start back up?"

"After Labor Day. Why?"

He turned a bit to get a better look at her. "Look, I need a new cook. Mine just quit. My last concert is July 30. My manager has started making inquiries for a replacement, but why make it hard when it could be simple? Would you consider being my cook on the tour? I'd give you a good salary and cover all your expenses."

Her legs wobbled like Jell-O. "Do you mind if I sit down?"

"Of course not."

She slid into the booth across from him and scrubbed her face with both hands, trying to wake up. "You're offering me a job?"

"Well, you're out of school. We could help each other."

Wow. Okay, this was a surprise. Tory rested her head on one hand. "God knows I need the money. I can't sell my family's house. It's a serious fixer upper. I inherited the mortgage and my grandfather's hospital bills when he died. And then the grant didn't come through for my research, and the tuition and loan payments keep coming due." She compressed her lips. "I must be tired. I don't usually babble."

Rye shifted in his seat like he was super uncomfortable. Who could blame him?

She rubbed her temples—his drumming was beating in time with the beginnings of a headache. "Tell me more about this job." Was she actually considering his offer? Was he really violent? He didn't seem to be.

"Our cross-country tour started ten days ago in Nashville and lasts until the end of the summer."

"What would I have to do?"

Rye shrugged and put down the fork. Finally!

"If you joined the tour, you'd be on my bus. You'd cook me three meals a day and have a day off every week." The salary he named made her jaw drop.

The thousand dollars he'd paid for dinner was peanuts in comparison. "You're kidding."

"I never joke about money. You'll earn every penny as my cook. I love to eat." He chuckled. "My last cook's pie couldn't compete with yours."

"You said your cook quit. Seems a little strange since you just started the tour—"

"Ten days ago," he finished, rubbing a hand over his goatee, grimacing. "Smart, aren't you? Well, I don't like to talk out of school, but she slept with someone in my band. It was a big mistake—for both of them. She heaved a chocolate cream pie at him on the way out. I'd need to know you wouldn't follow in her footsteps, so to speak."

"So all I have to do is cook for you three times a day and not sleep with anyone in your band?"

A dark laugh escaped. "Well, when you put it that way, it *does* sound like an unusual stipulation."

She turned sideways and drew her knees to her chest, crossing her ankles on the seat of the booth. "Well, that won't be too hard."

Rye hummed in his throat and reached for the fork. He started tapping again. The man couldn't sit still. Would it be rude to grab the fork and hide it?

"You haven't seen them yet—only me."

"Do they look like you?" Oops, did she just say that?

His head drew back sharply. The tapping stopped, thank God.

"I mean, do they look like cowboys?" she qualified.

He cleared his throat and glanced over her shoulder. Tory followed his gaze. Myra was watching them through the window in the kitchen door.

"Well, I guess so."

Tory waved a hand dismissively. "No problem then. Marlboro men don't appeal to me." They were attractive in an Alpha way, but she liked her men smart and sensitive, not afraid of their feelings.

He twirled the fork around. From the way his mouth was pinched, she could tell he hadn't liked her response. When he rapped the fork against the table again, she finally darted out a hand.

"Could you..."

He settled back against the booth and crossed his arms, but a few seconds later his foot started tapping. Did he have attention deficit disorder in addition to anger issues?

"So, are you game? It'll be tons of traveling. You'll see more of the great U.S. of A. than you've ever wanted. We have twenty-four more concerts in twenty-three states. It's a merry-go-round, but it can be fun. But you'll need to decide now. I'd like you to start tonight. We're heading out shortly to the next stop."

Now? That was like...

The kitchen door burst open and Myra bustled out, her panty hose making that awful rubbing sound, reminding Tory why she never wore them.

"Tory, you have to do it, honey. It's the answer to your prayers."

Tory wasn't so sure the big man upstairs bothered answering her prayers anymore. "You shouldn't be eavesdropping," she said, but there was no censure in her voice. She rubbed the tense muscles in her neck. "Anyway, I'm not so sure I should be considering this after recent events."

Myra's face turned red. "Well, I'm sure he had a good reason for pushing that man. Didn't you, Mr. Crenshaw?"

His nod was as stiff as her back.

Tory raised an eyebrow at him. "Nice to have such loyal fans, isn't it?" God, what kind of wild behavior would she witness? Her grandma had always warned her about things that sounded too good to be true...but the money. She'd be crazy to pass it up. It would go a long way toward solving her financial woes.

His stare didn't waver. "Myra, could you give us a second here?"

"Of course," she said, heading back into the kitchen without another word.

"You have something you want to ask me?" he growled once they were alone together.

Her fingers curled around the fork she'd taken from him. "Well...if I'm going to take the job, I need to be comfortable, I guess. I'd like to know that you had a good reason, like Myra thinks, that you aren't violent."

He didn't say anything for a long while, and the long seconds were marked by the tapping of his knee. Tory tried not to fidget under his angry stare.

"I'm not violent, and I had a good reason," he muttered.

When he didn't continue, she leaned forward. "And..."

He yanked on his ball cap again. "Christ, I miss my Stetson. Look, I don't have to tell you shit."

"You do if you want me to take the job."

He leaned his elbows on the table. "It was a family matter, all right?" he hissed. "It made me crazy upset, and I shoved that man out of my way when he got in my face. He fell and started yelling and...oh hell."

Tory pressed her lips together to keep from asking more questions. Myra talked about him all the time, giving her the latest updates from the tabloids. There had been no mention of his family in the news, and she knew he wasn't married. He was considered one of those famous sexy bachelors, and yet tonight he looked like a normal guy, much less arrogant and cocky than all those pictures in the tabloids. She studied him closer. She wasn't sure when it had happened in their conversation, but underneath the anger, there was hurt. His face had fallen. His color had gone from tan to pale. He looked away from her.

"I'm sorry," she said, lowering her voice.

He snorted. "Forget it. I'm a bad boy, honey, but I'm no criminal. Does that reassure you?"

"Okay, I'll do it." God help her, and then she remembered she wasn't convinced that God cared about people like her, the ones who'd lost everything. Her stomach jumped like a pond of frogs, excitement and terror warring inside her.

Rye stroked his goatee. "Good. The buses leave in about an hour," he said, telling her where to meet him. "I can stretch it to two, but we have another concert tomorrow night in Minneapolis. Now, go tell your friend, so you can get going."

Right. Tory darted into the kitchen. Myra was dancing an Irish jig when she walked through the door. "Oh my God! You'll be famous, Tory. Maybe this will help you get your cookbook published. Wouldn't your grandma love that?"

Could her grandma love that from heaven? She wasn't so sure, but she liked the idea. "I don't want fame, Myra. I only want the money."

Myra placed her hands on Tory's shoulders. "Everything's going to be fine now. You'll see. I'll take care of the house while you're gone. And when you figure out how your mail should be directed, let me know, and I'll forward it to you." She pulled Tory in for a hug. "You call and tell me how everything is going. Your grandma would get a kick out of this if she were still with us. Gosh, I still can't believe she's been gone three years."

Tears filled Tory's eyes, making the kitchen look like she was viewing it through a half-empty fish bowl. But she didn't let them run over. She'd almost mastered burying her emotions, but there were still hits and misses.

"Thanks, Myra. I wouldn't have gotten through any of this..." While taking care of her grandparents these past four years, she'd made few friends. All of her friends growing up had moved away for college. Myra's presence in her life had lessened the blow of not being able to socialize with people her own age.

Myra leaned back and framed Tory's face. "Your grandma helped me get my job at this diner when I was your age. I owe her. And it's not hard to look out for you, Tory."

"I need to go pack and make some arrangements," she said in a hoarse voice.

Myra kissed her cheek and then stepped back. "I'll talk to Mel tomorrow and let him know you won't be with us this summer. He'll be so happy for you, Tory. I heard him say how he wished he could pay you more. He loved your grandma like we all did."

"I feel like I'm leaving him in the lurch."

"Don't worry. I can't cook as good as you, but I can help out until he hires someone. Now, let's get you back to Rye Crenshaw. If I were twenty years younger, I'd fight you for this opportunity, dear."

Rye was standing by the door when they emerged.

Tory drew in a breath. "It's all so fast." And she'd have to call Connie Perkins, her realtor, in the morning to tell her what was happening.

"Life works that way sometimes," he said with an enigmatic smile. "Myra, it was a real pleasure." And he tipped his finger to his ball cap.

Myra pulled him into a hug.

Still in a daze—this was just about the last thing Tory had expected to happen when she woke up this morning—she followed Rye out to the parking lot. He stopped by an ugly car and dug out his keys.

"That's your ride?" Of all the things she'd imagined a famous singer might drive, a dented muscle car wasn't one of them.

"I borrowed it. I'm traveling on a tour bus, remember? Do you have a pen and piece of paper?"

She dug into her purse and handed over a grocery slip and ballpoint. He scribbled on the crumpled paper in bold strokes before handing them back.

"That's my cell if you have any trouble finding me. I'll tell

Clayton, my deputy, to keep an eye out for you. He handles all the hiring, so he'll go over all the details with you. Be there in two hours," he instructed, ducking into the car. His head hit the ceiling. Cursing, he slammed the door. The car turned over once before the engine started.

Tory had to bite her lip when it backfired as he reversed and left the parking lot. When she turned back toward the diner, Myra was standing in the doorway. She felt a shimmer of warmth crest over her. Myra's mothering had started when Tory was a kid, after her mom and dad died in a car crash. The diner, where her grandma had been the cook, had been her second home.

"I'll miss you." She dug into her pocket and counted out five bills. "Take half. I don't want to hear a word of protest."

Myra took the money and brushed a hand over her face to wipe away a tear. "Thank you. Do you want me to help you pack and give you a ride to the fairgrounds?"

"No, go on home. I have cab money, remember?"

Myra laughed and pulled her in for a hug. Tory relaxed into her embrace before breaking away and heading for her car.

The H in the diner's sign sputtered to life as she started the engine, making her halt. The word *Heaven* lit up for the first time in months before going dark again. Even with all her doubts, the sight sent a shock through her system. It seemed like an omen of something...she just wasn't sure what. Rubbing her arms, she climbed in her car and waved goodbye.

I hope you liked the excerpt. Can't you already see the sparks that are going to fly between Tory and Rye? If you want to keep reading, hop on over to your favorite retailer and buy COUNTRY HEAVEN. And just to tell you a little secret... Rye Crenshaw first appeared in my Dare Valley series, a connected series to Dare River, so I'll hope you'll check out his antics there as well. For more information about the rest of my books, keep reading. I'd love to hear what you think of this special cookbook in a review. Oh, and as I mentioned, I have a COUNTRY HEAVEN SONGBOOK available as well. Hope you check it out.

Coming Soon

The Dare Valley Series continues...

Book 6: THE PARK OF SUNSET DREAMS

Jane Wilcox and Matthew Hale's story

Available Spring 2014

Also Coming Soon

The Dare River Series continues...

Book 2: THE CHOCOLATE GARDEN

Tammy Morrison and John Parker McGuiness' story

Available Summer 2014

Other Books By Ava

All books can be enjoyed as a stand-alone if this is your first time reading. Enjoy!

Dare Valley Series

NORA ROBERTS LAND

Meredith and Tanner's story

A journalist returns to her hometown to debunk the Nora Roberts' romance novels her ex-husband blamed for their divorce only to discover happy endings exist when she falls for a hero straight out of a bona fide romance novel.

FRENCH ROAST
Jill and Brian's story
A small-town girl mixes business and pleasure with her childhood BFF until his own Mrs. Robinson returns, making her question their friendship and their newfound love.

THE GRAND OPENING
Peggy and Mac's story
A cynical single-mom cop discovers she can't bluff her way out of love when a mysterious poker-playing hotel magnate shows her it's worth the gamble.

THE HOLIDAY SERENADE
Abbie and Rhett's story
A professional gambler prepares a holiday serenade to convince a single mom and Martha Stewart wannabe to give their love a second chance.

THE TOWN SQUARE
Harriet and Arthur's story
An ambitious journalist returns to Dare Valley to start a newspaper empire, but is soon caught up with his mysterious secretary, not realizing she's come to his small town for revenge.

ABOUT THE AUTHOR

USA Today Bestselling Author Ava Miles burst onto the contemporary romance scene after receiving Nora Roberts' blessing for her use of Ms. Roberts' name in her debut novel, *NORA ROBERTS LAND*, which kicked off The Dare Valley Series and brought praise from reviewers and readers alike. Much to Ava's delight, *USA Today* Contributor Becky Lower selected it as one of the Best Books of the Year. Ava continued The Dare Valley Series in *FRENCH ROAST*, which Tome Tender says "raised the entertainment bar again" and then *THE GRAND OPENING*, which reviewer Mary J. Gramlich says "is a continuation of love, family, and relationships." The next books in the series, *THE HOLIDAY SERENADE*, was met with high praise and her ode to the early 1960s, *THE TOWN SQUARE*, what she calls *Mad Men* in a small town with a happy ending, melted reader's hearts.

Ava based her original series on a family newspaper, modeled after her own. Her great-great grandfather won it in a poker game in 1892, so Ava is no stranger to adventurous men and models her heroes after men like that—or like Tim McGraw, her favorite country music singer. Now Ava shares the Dare River series, set in the deep South, telling the story of a country singer and a beautiful cook. A former chef herself, Ava used her culinary background to infuse the story with family and personal recipes, but she also used her love for music to write country music songs to set the stage in the novel, creating a unique book experience. Ava—a writer since childhood—now lives in her own porch-swinging-friendly community with an old-fashioned Main Street lined with small businesses.

If you'd like more information about Ava Miles and her upcoming books, visit www.avamiles.com and connect to Ava on Facebook, Twitter, and Pinterest.

Made in the USA
Las Vegas, NV
03 November 2023

80188353R00039